1

POEMS

& LOVE

LETTERS

from

GOD

3

THIS BOOK

is

DEDICATED

to

The Blessed, Broken, and Beyond…

Remember, God loves you.

"As Jesus came up out of the water, he saw the
heavens split apart and the Holy Spirit descending
on him like a dove. And a voice from heaven said,
"You are my dearly loved Son, and you bring me
great joy."

Mark 1:10-11 NLT

Tananda Parson

POEMS
& LOVE
LETTERS

from

GOD

Abandoned

Trampled over and over again
When you left me to die
Physically and emotionally
My mind can't process the reason why
Neglected from the beginning
before you knew who I was
You made a selfish decision
that left me deeply scarred

Waiting….

Waiting for someone to choose me
Hoping for someone to love me
Yearning to be seen for who I really am

Wanting to receive the love of one specific man

But how would you know this?

You're a coward who ran astray

You couldn't see the pain you caused

When you chose to cast me away

Betrayed prematurely before I could make a sound
in the earth

Rejected before you could get to know me or know
my worth

Tormented by abandon for so many years

Living empty, numb, bitter, and quietly unfulfilled

Until....

Until one day the stars align, and we stand face to
face

Perhaps, you got lost or God arranged it so that we
would occupy the very same space

Would you open your mouth and try to somehow explain?

Would you beg for my forgiveness or hang your head in shame?

Could I watch while you hurt?

Maybe even laugh while you weep

Let revenge run its course

Despite my heart so big and my love so deep

No!!!

Of course, I wouldn't!

My heart has changed toward you

I now know I am not alone

The hurt and betrayal is gone

I couldn't bear to put you through the same pain

When you left me behind

I wouldn't dare harm you or treat you unkind.

Now forgiven and free

You get the healed version of me
Desperate to get to know you,
I've cast the rejection aside
With just a glimpse of hope
And not a measure of pride
I'd pour out my heart
With arms open wide
Embracing the now
Leaving the past behind
Forever grateful and fully satisfied
To make room for you in my life.

"…for he has said, *I will never leave you and I will never abandon you.* " So we can feel sure to say, *"The Lord is my helper, and I will not be afraid. What can people do to me?"*

Hebrews 13:5-6 NET

Dear Barren Daughter,

You are Loved. I know you think you are inadequate or not enough. But what you carry, I gave to you. All that you have was made by my hands. The broken womb you carry is whole in my eyes. Press on to see the goodness in what I have created for you. No sooner will you lose hope when I have delivered all I have promised. Just like Hannah who cried out to me. Your blessing will come in the appointed time. My appointed time.

Love,

The Promise Keeper

"And in due time she gave birth to a son. She named him Samuel for she said, "I asked the Lord for him."

1 Samuel 1: 20 NLT

"Sir, do you remember me?" Hannah asked. "I am the very woman who stood here several years ago praying to the lord. I asked the Lord to give me this boy and he has granted my request."

1 Samuel 1:26-27 NLT

Broken

Turned from left to right

Held in the potter's hand

Flipped upside down

Then right side up again

Cracked and chipped

Broken but not destroyed

You are being held in the potter's hands

Carefully placed on the potter's wheel

Delicately molded and shaped

Back into your rightful place

All cracks filled in

All chips erased

No more broken pieces

Shattered from this life

But now made whole again

Put back together

By His skillful hands

My Beautiful Creation,

I knew exactly how to push you. And where to apply enough pressure. Now a brand-new creation, ready to be used by me.

No longer broken. No longer scarred

Better than what you were. You are now whole again.

Love,

The Potter

"Yet we who have this spiritual treasure are like common clay pots, in order to show that the supreme power belongs to God, not to us. We are often troubled, but not crushed; sometimes in doubt, but never in despair; there are many enemies, but we are never without a friend; and though badly hurt at times, we are not destroyed."

2 Corinthians 4:7-9 GNT

Dependent

Lean on Me, trust in Me

Give me your heart's desires

Watch how I make them a reality

All that you need is here in Me

Lean on Me, trust in Me

I'll always be right here

That's my guarantee

Lean on Me, trust in Me

Wherever you stand

There I will be

If ever you fall or scrape a knee

Like a loving parent I'll rescue you

Lean on Me, trust in Me

It's in my hands

Whatever you lack

Just ask your wealthy Father

I've always got your back

Lean on Me, trust in Me

I have everything you need

It's just waiting to be released

If only you would come to me

If only I was the one you chose to seek

Lean on Me, trust in Me

I'm not hard to find

I'm not hidden away

I'm right hear eagerly waiting

To listen to whatever you have to say

Lean on Me, trust in Me

I'm the only partner that never leaves

I have everything you'll ever need

It's Me and you against the world

Together we'll conquer and always defeat

Lean on Me, Trust in Me

"Continue to ask, and God will give to you. Continue to search, and you will find. Continue to knock, and the door will open for you. Yes, everyone who continues asking will receive. He who continues searching will find. And he who continues knocking will have the door opened for him."

Matthew 7:7-8 ICB

"Trust in the Lord with all your heart. Never rely on what you think you know. Remember the Lord in everything you do, and he will show you the right way."

Proverbs 3:5-6 GNT

Divorced

Crushed. Done. Period.

Whole life uprooted

Turned upside down

Blindsided. Numb.

Why didn't I see this coming?

Why did this happen to me?

All the judgmental stares

Was it my fault?

How did I get here?

Why did I get married in the first place?

No more honesty and trust

No longer wed to my love

Just me, myself, and I

Reservation for a party of one!

Who wants to be alone again?

Come home to an empty house?

Who wants to lie in a lonely bed?

Could I start my life over?

Where would I begin?

Am I still capable of love?

Who will love me now?

⁂

I will," says the Lord

I always have and I always will

Place your lonely, broken heart in my capable hands.

Let me heal you from the inside out.

Let me touch the places you hide away from others

Let me hold you when you're sad

Let me calm your anger

Let's start over together

Let's remove your fear

It's not so scary when I am here

Who will love you now?

"I will," says the Lord

I always have and I always will

Love,

Your Covenant Partner

"Be strong. Take courage. Don't be intimidated. Don't give them a second thought because God, your God, is striding ahead of you. He's right there with you. He won't let you down; he won't leave you."

Deuteronomy 31:6 MSG

Doubtful

How will it happen for me?

I can't see how it will come to pass

It's hard to believe in a future I just can't see

When my past has been so bleak

Am I even worthy to receive?

All that I desire or all that I need.

Have I done enough good?

To earn the blessings, I seek

Where are all the rewarding things

I've prayed diligently for

Why have I been face to face

With every closed and locked door

I can't see how it will happen for me

I've failed so many times

It's hard for me to believe

It's hard to have faith

When doubt is all I see

~~~~~

Did you know that with a friend like me, you have all you'll ever need? Place your eyes only on me. Release the doubt as we move forward to all I have for you. Let the past go. That's not who you are anymore. Failure is not my plan for your life. You have a renewed mind, heart, and spirit. And Me to guide you into the abundant life I have for you. Don't doubt the God who knows, sees, and has all you need. Walk forward in faith and cast your cares upon me.

-The God Who Sees

"But when you ask for something, you must have faith and not doubt. Anyone who doubts is like an ocean wave tossed around in a storm. If you are that kind of person, you can't make up your mind, and you surely can't be trusted. So don't expect the Lord to give you anything at all."

James 1:6-8 CEV

Fading Fire

A flicker replaced your burning flame
Tingles and butterflies long forgotten
When the love you share has faded
Remember the purposes and reasons
The memories that brought you here
Feelings and emotions you shared
Stop passing like ships in the night
Come back together with intention
Pause to gaze in each other's eyes
Let yourself get lost in their scent
Delve into their innermost being
All you need is that one spark
A flicker of light to fill the dark
Rekindle that flame
Dig deep until you find it again

You're not the person you were before
Rediscover who you are now
Reach for each other and relearn the reason you
chose to make the covenant vow.

Marriage is sacred and important to me. Why waste it, why squander it away? Take the time to love one another the way that I love you. Fulfill the needs of each other unselfishly. It will bring you joy to watch them smile and light up at the affection you show. Pray through the hard times. Remember why I joined you together. I don't make mistakes.

Love,

God

"The look in your eyes, my sweetheart and bride,

and the necklace you are wearing have stolen my

heart. Your love delights me,

my sweetheart and bride.

Your love is better than wine;

your perfume more fragrant than any spice."

Song of Solomon 4:9-10 GNT

"Close your heart to every love but mine; hold no

one in your arms but me. Love is as powerful as

death; passion is as strong as death itself.

It bursts into flame and burns like a raging fire.

Water cannot put it out, no flood can drown it. But

if any tried to buy love with their wealth, contempt

is all they would get."

Song of Solomon 8:6-7 GNT

From Here to There

I'm at my wit's end

I've done all that I can do

There's nowhere left for me to turn

There's nothing left for me to do

The road is too long

The river is too deep

The mountain is too high

I'm just too weak

My feet are tired and worn

My strength has completely gone

So here I sit

Along this journey of my life

A stone's throw from the finish line

Or maybe it's a mile

I just can't tell

Dismayed and confused?

How did I come this far, just to fail?

My daughter, My son

This is not how you will win

Your success is not in how you run

It's upon whom you choose to depend

It's from where you draw your strength

Whether at the start, middle or end

I'm there when a step seems too hard to take

We'll pause for just a moment

Let's call it a short break

Take a few deep breaths

See, we're still in the race

The road is not so long
The mountain is not too high
Let's take it one step at a time
I'll carry you if I need to
No matter what it takes
I won't let you give up right here
You're going to finish this race
We'll run from here to there
Across the finish line
Together side-by-side.
Love,
The Finisher

"I have fought the good fight. I have finished the race. I have kept the faith."

2 Timothy 4:7 NIRV

"God began doing a good work in you. And he will continue it until it is finished when Jesus Christ comes again. I am sure of that."

Philippians 1:6 ICB

Dear Fully Focused

You've made me so proud

Just to think of what you could have done, but you chose me

To think of where you could have gone, but you chose me

Just to think of how you could have slipped, but you chose me

To think of how that thing could have distracted you, but you chose me

You didn't lie down or sell your soul

You didn't compromise because I'm in control

It is I who orchestrate your life from the moment you are conceived

Your will tries to resist but my plans always succeed

Keep focusing on the things above and keep your mind clear

Until the appointed time comes don't give in to the fear

Fear of loneliness

Fear of rejection

Fear of missing out

You will see at just the right moment

How blessings start pouring out

You'll get all the things I promised

When you choose faith and not doubt

Until then, keep praying, keep fasting, and keep putting me first

I see you and I won't let you down.

I am proud of you.

I love you.

-God

"I want you to live as free of complications as possible. When you're unmarried, you're free to concentrate on simply pleasing the Master. Marriage involves you in all the nuts and bolts of domestic life and in wanting to please your spouse, leading to so many more demands on your attention. The time and energy that married people spend on caring for and nurturing each other, the unmarried can spend in becoming whole and holy instruments of God. I'm trying to be helpful and make it as easy as possible for you, not make things harder. All I want is for you to be able to develop a way of life in which you can spend plenty of time together with the Master without a lot of distractions."

1 Corinthians 7:32-35 MSG

Dear Heartbroken One,

I love you. I watched the light grow dim and fade from your eyes. Your desire and drive came to a halt. Your heart has been crushed by another careless hand. Dropped over and over until you feel unrecognizable. Mishandled by hands not meant to carry you. Running from the past. Hiding in plain sight. But I still see you.

The you who I created. Fierce and strong. Mighty and tall. Confident with grace. It has not gone away. It's just covered by years of looking and longing for a love like mine. Here I am, run back to my open arms. I've been right here waiting, all along.

Love,

God

"The Lord your God wins victory after victory and is always with you. He celebrates and sings because of you, and he will refresh your life with his love. The LORD has promised: Your sorrow has ended, and you can celebrate."

Zephaniah 3:17-20 CEV

Hopeful

Things don't look how you want them to
It didn't go how you thought it would go
How do you move keep moving holding on to what
you're hoping for?
How do you get past the let down and
disappointment of not seeing what you wanted to
see?
Not getting what you thought you would get? Not
going the places, you thought you would go?
Selah.
All that I've promised will surely come to pass.
Take hold of my hand and continue to walk. When
the right doors open, we'll walk through them
together. The right opportunities will arise, and
we'll conquer each one. I am all the faith and hope

you need to get where you're destined to go. Trust in me, that I won't let you down. That I won't keep you from the good I have planned for you. I may hold you back until it's time to propel you forward. I may hide you away until it's time to reveal the masterpiece I've created in you. Place your faith, hope, and trust in Me and we'll get there on the right day, at the right time, and at the exact moment you are supposed to be there.

Love,

The Timekeeper

"But it is just as the Scriptures say, "What God has planned for people who love him is more than eyes have seen or ears have heard. It has never even entered our minds!"

1 Corinthians 2:9 CEV

Dear Hurt,

Disgraced and dismissed, my feelings disregarded
Pushed away, tossed aside
As if (insert name) didn't matter
I have but one choice, one final desperate move
And that is to fight to permanently get over you
My freedom held over the fire for way too long
Mentally paralyzed by memories, replaying a sad
song
Threatened by the truth revealing itself
Needing to break free from your grip of death
You tormented and wounded my ego, pride, and
self-esteem
I was crippled by your weight, never able to reach
my dream

I've finally realized your power was hidden in my fear

But there's no more vacancy

HURT, can no longer live here.

You don't control me anymore!

Take all your baggage,

You're out the door!

Gone are the chains of guilt and shame

I'm totally healed in Jesus' name!

I'm not that prisoner you abused and scorned

I've been released and set free

Like a phoenix reborn.

"But to you who are willing to listen, I say, love your enemies! Do good to those who hate you. Bless those who curse you. Pray for those who hurt you."

Luke 6:27-28 NLT

Loss

"It gets easier," they say

The pain will subside

The aching in your heart

Will go away someday

This unbearable tragedy

Whether expected or surprise

Is a moment in time

You just cannot see past

God, why did you take them?

God, why couldn't they stay?

God, why would you do this to me?

God why would you put me through all this pain?

God, how could you allow this to happen?

God, why didn't you save them?
God, why?

My child,
I knew their end from their beginning
And my plans will always prevail
You needed more time with them
But my purpose for their life has been fulfilled
Right now, you can't understand
Or see the point of it all
The grief is too great

The hurt has taken control

The wound is much too deep

Remember my grace is enough

And I'll be waiting right here

Take my hand when you're ready

To let them go and finally grieve

To walk through this pain

I'm the comforter you need

The answers that you seek

Won't bring you peace

You need a safe place to heal

You'll only find that place in me

"If you are tired from carrying heavy burdens, come to me and I will give you rest."

Matthew 11:28 CEV

Dear Mid-Life Crisis,

Bread gets stale. But even croutons have their place in this world. There is nothing I've made that I can't make new again. Let me reinvent you. Not with fancy cars, new clothes, and ridiculous wealth. But with my wisdom on how to navigate this phase of your life. Trust me to know your future and to make it good. Time is not slipping away. For my timing is perfect. Trust me. I know what I'm doing. Lean on me and I will give you understanding. Don't panic. Just rest in me. I have exactly what you need. That new thing that you're looking for, it's already inside of you. Let me bring it out the right way at the right time.

Love,

God

"My child, don't lose sight of the common sense and discernment.

Hang on to them, for they will refresh your soul. They are like jewels on a necklace. They keep you safe on your way, and your feet will not stumble. You can go to bed without fear; you will lie down and sleep soundly. You need not be afraid of sudden disaster or the destruction that comes upon the wicked, for the Lord is your security. He will keep your foot from being caught in a trap."

Proverbs 3:21-26 NLT

Dear Newlyweds,

You are so loved.

Look at all you've been given. The fruits of my labor. To receive such a precious gift. A covenant connection with another soul designed specifically for you. Cherish this gift. Cover them in prayer and wash them with My word. Never take for granted all that you've been given. Stay devoted to one another and keep their name on your lips. Think it not strange that two have now become one. Depend on each other, lean on one another, and place your union always in my hands. Seek me in every area of your marriage. Be vulnerable and compassionate with one another. Leave the rest to Me.

Love,

God

"Wives, follow the lead of your own husbands as you follow the Lord. The husband is the head of the wife, just as Christ is the head of the church. The church is Christ's body. He is its Savior. The church follows the lead of Christ. In the same way, wives should follow the lead of their husbands in everything."

Ephesians 5: 22-23 NIRV

"In the same way, husbands should love their wives.

They should love them as they love their own

bodies. Any man who loves his wife loves himself.

After all, no one ever hated their own body. Instead,

they feed and care for their body. And this is what

Christ does for the church. We are parts of his body.

Scriptures says, "That's why a man will leave his

father and mother and be joined to his wife. The

two will become one." ...A husband also must love

his wife. He must love her just as he loves himself.

And must respect her husband"

Ephesians 5:28-31; 33 NIRV

Overwhelmed

I've poured out all I have

I've got nothing left to give

My mind is spent and strained

I've given all I can give

I'm empty, lost, and weak

Searching....

Searching for a place

Any place to rest

A place to refill me

A moment to be refreshed

Pulled in every direction

Drained of every breath

Left without a single lifeline

Is this emotional, physical, or spiritual death?

~~~~

My child,

I've watched you run yourself in the ground. Being everything to everyone. Until you're tired and sick. With all the run down, where are all the people you gave your last to? Where are the hungry hands that picked and pulled at you? Who's left behind to fill you back up? Who's willing and ready to overflow your empty cup?

Come. Rest in Me. I have all the strength you need

Let Me be their God, point them towards me. Your life purpose and plan are to trust in me. If they're empty, hurt, or broken, just like you, I'll make them complete.

Lay your head on my chest, I'll clean up the mess.

Rest in Me my child.

Love,

God

"The Lord gives strength to those who are tired. He gives more power to those who are weak."

Isaiah 40:29 ICB

"Yes, I must find my rest in God. He is the God who gives me hope. It is surely true that he is my rock and the God who saves me. He is like a fort to me, so I will always be secure. I depend on God to save me and to honor me. He is my mighty rock and my place of safety. Trust in him at all times, you people. Tell him all your troubles. God is our place of safety."

Psalm 62:5-8 NIRV

Puppy Love

Your heart is open for the first time

The roses smell different

The sky looks bluer

The grass is so much greener

The object of your affection

Just noticed you were alive

Butterflies fluttering inside

Daydreams stealing your time

Sleep is not an option

Counting the hours and minutes

Until you see them again

Life now has new meaning

Your world is forever changed

From this day forward

Your eyes have been opened to love

Now, nothing else is more important

But...

That has always been my heart towards you

Every time I have a fleeting thought of you

My heart smiles

This is my creation that I formed with my hands

A delicate jewel I created from the ground

The longer I stare at you, the more my love shows

Let your passion for me grow stronger than for anyone else

I delight when we come together and spend quality time

My love never fades, and my passion never goes away

Let's do this again and again, every chance you get.

Remember, no matter where you are,

I love you best.

Love,

God

"And I pray that you and all God's holy people will have the power to understand the greatness of Christ's love. I pray that you can understand how wide and how long and how high and how deep that love is. Christ's love is greater than any person can ever know. But I pray that you will be able to know that love. Then you can be filled with the fullness of God."

Ephesians 3:18-19 ICB

Triggered

What you carry deep inside

What no one sees

What you try to hide

Lay it all at my feet

This time around we'll win

No more defeat

Don't suffer alone

I'm always here

You think I'm far

But I'm always near

The emotion, the shame

The bitterness, the pain

I see all the memories that rush in

They flood your brain

I saw what happened

Every rise and fall

But this time, give it to Me

I want it all

No more flashbacks that bring pain

No more being ashamed

Pour it all out on me

I can take it away

No more heavy guilt for you to carry

Because I've made you free

Trust me enough to leave it here

Every thought, every burden

Every worry, every care

So, when the thoughts arise

You have exactly what you need

I've taken away the tears

Now I leave you with my peace

"Three different times I begged God to make me well again. Each time he said, "No. But I am with you; that is all you need. My power shows up best in weak people." Now I am glad to boast about how weak I am; I am glad to be a living demonstration of Christ's power, instead of showing off my own power and abilities."

2 Corinthians 12:8-9 TLB

True Love's Kiss

Why haven't I been found

Am I not worthy of love?

I'm tired of being alone

Am I just not worthy enough?

Will I ever create my happy home?

When I've finally wed another

Bring forth brand new life

Will I become a mother? A father?

Look at me…

My love record is spotless

My dating resume is clean

I've put in all the work

Nothing left to do behind the scenes

I go to work, I go to church

No extra play time for me

No slip ups or fall downs

Yet I'm still waiting to be found

Where is my Queen?

Where is my Mr. Right?

I'm here where I've been your whole lifetime

Shaping and molding you for just the right one

I'm in no hurry, for in due time

Your eyes will meet my appointed son

The man I chose to pursue my beloved daughter

The woman I've kept hidden in her closet

Praying to me about her heart's desires

The one who knows that good gifts come from the heavenly father

The one I created for you, will love you inside and out

You'll know when they find you, so get rid of your doubt

Just continue to wait because you don't want to miss

When two hearts become one and finally share true love's kiss

Love,

The Real Matchmaker

"As the bridegroom was delayed, they all became drowsy and slept. But at midnight there was a cry, 'Here is the bridegroom! Come out to meet him.'

… the bridegroom came, and those who were ready went in with him to the marriage feast, and the door was shut.

Watch therefore, for you know neither the day nor the hour."

Matthew 25: 5-6;10;13 ESV

Dear God,

I feel like you are the only one who truly loves me. Why do I feel like I have to work to make people love me? I don't know how to find real love.

Love,
Your Lost child

<hr>

My Child,

I do love you, but there are others who love you too. Let them love you. Accept it with open arms. Be vulnerable, your true authentic self. They'll love you like I do.

But God, I don't know how to accept it.

I'll show you how. You show up being who you think they want to see; that's people pleasing. I didn't create you for them, I created you for me. Let me show you real love.

Love,

Your Heavenly Father

"This is real love—not that we loved God, but that he loved us and sent his Son as a sacrifice to take away our sins."

1 John 4:10 NLT

"My commandment is this—

to **love one another** just as I have **loved you.**"

John 15:12 NET